A Mind of Winter

POEMS FOR A SNOWY SEASON

Selected by ROBERT ATWAN

Introduction by
DONALD HALL

Beacon Press

Boston

BEACON PRESS
25 Beacon Street
Boston, Massachusetts 02108-2892
www.beacon.org

Beacon Press books are published under the auspices of
the Unitarian Universalist Association of Congregations.

15 14 13 12 11   8 7 6 5 4 3 2 1

This book is printed on acid-free paper that meets the uncoated
paper ANSI/NISO specifications for permanence as revised in 1992.

Illustrations by Thomas Nason reproduced with permission

Text design by Christopher Kuntze

LIBRARY OF CONGRESS CATALOGING-IN-PUBLICATION DATA

A mind of winter : poems for a snowy season / selected by Robert Atwan ; introduction
by Donald Hall.
        p. cm.
    ISBN 978-0-8070-6920-2 (acid-free paper)
        1. Winter—Poetry. 2. American poetry—New England. 3. New England—Poetry.
    I. Atwan, Robert

PS595.W5 M56 2002
811.008'033—dc21   2002066575

CONTENTS

Introduction: Winter Again

Winter is always again. From the fire of October, so garish it would be vulgar if it were design, the year extends through diminishing sun into the grays and browns of an analytic cubist landscape. One day the matted leaves take on a white, gradual thickening. Snow decorates the tops of boulders and the flat extent of hay fields. It reverses the twilight shades of November into multiple curves of white, against which deciduous trunks raise their bare verticals, and continuous coniferous green takes on more green.

Winter is energy. Summer ranges from comfort to an annoyance of mosquitoes and lethargy.

Winter is the glad warmth of the parlor against the ground of ice. In John Greenleaf Whittier's "Snow-Bound," being snowbound has its comforts. Snow is comfortable unless we work in it. In the old days men chopped wood at twenty below zero against next year's cold, or sawed ice from river and pond against the coming summer.

The best part of winter is snow falling. Sky grays over, formidable in its warnings, and clouds blacken, until the first flutter falls. Flakes gather density until the frigid air is a white fabric of descent. Descent is the music of snow, proceeding to its coda, flat over garden and road and hay field. We sit on the porch, as long as we can stand it, to witness this falling.

The best part of winter is sun on the snow. We blink and our eyes water. The sun never shows so bright as it does in January's winter fields.

The best part of winter is the full moon on snowfields. It turns the landscape lunar, bumps and hollows unified by an uncanny light, which bounces from fields outside, upward to tin ceilings. "You could read a newspaper by it," we tell each other.

The best part of winter is imagining spring. Walking in whiteness that feathers to our boot tops, we dream awake that the days of April already warm us. We look through the surface of the humped white garden to watch daffodils rise, and peonies petalled the color of snow.

Winter is our bear-sleep of commodious shelter. Winter is the year's pause. The mind of winter studies desolation's purity, vigor, and strict beauty.

At winter's stuttering end, in March, midnight freezes and noon is tropical, maple trees grow tin pails, and from sugar houses smoke rises day and night. Winter springs into sweetness.

Maybe we northerners love snow because we are residual Calvinists. We luxuriate in darkness and deprivation. The descendants of Cotton Mather, the progeny of Martin Luther, we grasp suffering as our just reward. We bathe in absence. We return the embrace of ice. Do we Original Sinners deserve better, in our frozen city on the hill? We sing of snow to brag of pain.

Whatever the motives, poets dive into snow. Emerson delighted in "the frolic architecture of the snow," in which "the whited air / Hides hills and woods, the river, and the heaven . . . / In a tumultuous privacy of storm." For Longfellow snow was "the poem of the air, / Slowly in silent syllables recorded."

Poets continue their diving. Snow, says Mary Oliver, "shines like a field / of white flowers." In Richard Wilbur's eyes, ". . . night is all a settlement of snow." Robert Frost famously stopped by woods on a snowy evening, and on another occasion watched "the cottages in a row / Up to their shining eyes in snow." For Frost, sometimes snow is a desert place, but mostly he likes it. However, the great New England poet spent his winters in Miami.

A Mind of Winter

The Snow Man

One must have a mind of winter
To regard the frost and the boughs
Of the pine-trees crusted with snow;

And have been cold a long time
To behold the junipers shagged with ice,
The spruces rough in the distant glitter

Of the January sun; and not to think
Of any misery in the sound of the wind,
In the sound of a few leaves,

Which is the sound of the land
Full of the same wind
That is blowing in the same bare place

For the listener, who listens in the snow,
And, nothing himself, beholds
Nothing that is not there and the nothing that is.

ROSANNA WARREN

Snow Day

I have nothing to say on a white afternoon
but there are the candlesticks, etched,
hieratic, guarding the pane
with arching wicks; and there is the bottle of glue, and there
squirming upward, one black curlycue
succeeding another, the jungle plant on the window sill.
The life in this room is still.
There is nothing, nothing to do
about tonnage of snow in New
Haven, or
bells that won't ring downstairs at the door
or bells, in the tower, that will.
Nothing to say, except here,
discretely, we are
shaped in the dark in a darkening room
against the snow window, against the snow day.
And I think

of my friend, who was
not really my friend,
except for the death in her eyes, which were round
and wise like a turtle's.
I think of my friend and the snow, because
of that blank haven she found

when the Buick spun into her last snow day
on Route whatever-it-was, toward nightfall, and she
had no way to say what it was that she knew
with glass in her eyes and her mouth full of snow.

Year's End

Now winter downs the dying of the year,
And night is all a settlement of snow;
From the soft street the rooms of houses show
A gathered light, a shapen atmosphere,
Like frozen-over lakes whose ice is thin
And still allows some stirring down within.

I've known the wind by water banks to shake
The late leaves down, which frozen where they fell
And held in ice as dancers in a spell
Fluttered all winter long into a lake;
Graved on the dark in gestures of descent,
They seemed their own most perfect monument.

There was perfection in the death of ferns
Which laid their fragile cheeks against the stone
A million years. Great mammoths overthrown
Composedly have made their long sojourns,
Like palaces of patience, in the gray
And changeless lands of ice. And at Pompeii

The little dog lay curled and did not rise
But slept the deeper as the ashes rose
And found the people incomplete, and froze
The random hands, the loose unready eyes

Of men expecting yet another sun
To do the shapely thing they had not done.

These sudden ends of time must give us pause.
We fray into the future, rarely wrought
Save in the tapestries of afterthought.
More time, more time. Barrages of applause
Come muffled from a buried radio.
The New-year bells are wrangling with the snow.

It sifts from Leaden Sieves

It sifts from Leaden Sieves –
It powders all the Wood.
It fills with Alabaster Wool
The Wrinkles of the Road –

It makes an Even Face
Of Mountain, and of Plain –
Unbroken Forehead from the East
Unto the East again –

It reaches to the Fence –
It wraps it Rail by Rail
Till it is lost in Fleeces –
It deals Celestial Vail

To Stump, and Stack – and Stem –
A Summer's empty Room –
Acres of Joints, where Harvests were,
Recordless, but for them –

It Ruffles Wrists of Posts
As Ankles of a Queen –
Then stills its Artisans – like Ghosts –
Denying they have been –

Wind and Window Flower

Lovers, forget your love,
    And list to the love of these,
She a window flower,
    And he a winter breeze.

When the frosty window veil
    Was melted down at noon,
And the cagèd yellow bird
    Hung over her in tune,

He marked her through the pane,
    He could not help but mark,
And only passed her by,
    To come again at dark.

He was a winter wind,
    Concerned with ice and snow,
Dead weeds and unmated birds,
    And little of love could know.

But he sighed upon the sill,
    He gave the sash a shake,
As witness all within
    Who lay that night awake.

Perchance he half prevailed
    To win her for the flight
From the firelit looking-glass
    And warm stove-window light.

But the flower leaned aside
    And thought of naught to say,
And morning found the breeze
    A hundred miles away.

A Winter Twilight

A silence slipping around like death,
Yet chased by a whisper, a sigh, a breath;
One group of trees, lean, naked and cold,
Inking their crest 'gainst a sky green-gold;
One path that knows where the corn flowers were;
Lonely, apart, unyielding, one fir;
And over it softly leaning down,
One star that I loved ere the fields went brown.

Red Slippers

Red slippers in a shop-window; and outside in the street,
flaws of gray, windy sleet!

Behind the polished glass the slippers hang in long threads
of red, festooning from the ceiling like stalactites of blood,
flooding the eyes of passers-by with dripping color, jamming
their crimson reflections against the windows of cabs and
tram-cars, screaming their claret and salmon into the teeth
of the sleet, plopping their little round maroon lights upon
the tops of umbrellas.

The row of white, sparkling shop-fronts is gashed and
bleeding, it bleeds red slippers. They spout under the
electric light, fluid and fluctuating, a hot rain—and freeze
again to red slippers, myriadly multiplied in the mirror
side of the window.

They balance upon arched insteps like springing bridges of
crimson lacquer; they swing up over curved heels like
whirling tanagers sucked in a wind-pocket; they flatten out,
heelless, like July ponds, flared and burnished by red
rockets.

Snap, snap, they are cracker sparks of scarlet in the white,
monotonous block of shops.

They plunge the clangor of billions of vermilion trumpets into the crowd outside, and echo in faint rose over the pavement.

People hurry by, for these are only shoes, and in a window farther down is a big lotus bud of cardboard, whose petals open every few minutes and reveal a wax doll, with staring bead eyes and flaxen hair, lolling awkwardly in its flower chair.

One has often seen shoes, but whoever saw a cardboard lotus bud before?

The flaws of gray, windy sleet beat on the shop-window where there are only red slippers.

Winter Night

The church is an iceberg.

It's the wind. It must be blowing tonight
Out of those galactic orchards,
Their Copernican pits and stones.

The monster created by the mad Dr. Frankenstein
Sailed for the New World,
And ended up some place like New Hampshire.

Actually, it's just a local drunk,
Knocking with a snow shovel,
Wanting to go in and warm himself.

An iceberg, the book says, is a large drifting
Piece of ice, broken off a glacier.

JAMES RUSSELL LOWELL

The First Snow-Fall

The snow had begun in the gloaming,
    And busily all the night
Had been heaping field and highway
    With a silence deep and white.

Every pine and fir and hemlock
    Wore ermine too dear for an earl,
And the poorest twig on the elm-tree
    Was ridged inch deep with pearl.

From sheds new-roofed with Carrara
    Came Chanticleer's muffled crow,
The stiff rails softened to swan's-down,
    And still fluttered down the snow.

I stood and watched by the window
    The noiseless work of the sky,
And the sudden flurries of snow-birds,
    Like brown leaves whirling by.

I thought of a mound in sweet Auburn
    Where a little headstone stood;
How the flakes were folding it gently,
    As did robins the babes in the wood.

Up spoke our own little Mabel,
    Saying, "Father, who makes it snow?"
And I told of the good All-father
    Who cares for us here below.

Again I looked at the snow-fall,
    And thought of the leaden sky
That arched o'er our first great sorrow,
    When that mound was heaped so high.

I remembered the gradual patience
    That fell from that cloud like snow,
Flake by flake, healing and hiding
    The scar that renewed our woe.

And again to the child I whispered,
    "The snow that busheth all,
Darling, the merciful Father
    Alone can make it fall!"

Then, with eyes that saw not, I kissed her;
    And she, kissing back, could not know
That *my* kiss was given to her sister,
    Folded close under deepening snow.

GJERTRUD SCHNACKENBERG

The Paperweight

The scene within the paperweight is calm,
A small white house, a laughing man and wife,
Deep snow. I turn it over in my palm
And watch it snowing in another life,

Another world, and from this scene learn what
It is to stand apart: she serves him tea
Once and forever, dressed from head to foot
As she is always dressed. In this toy, history

Sifts down through the glass like snow, and we
Wonder if her single deed tells much
Or little of the way she loves, and whether he
Sees shadows in the sky. Beyond our touch,

Beyond our lives, they laugh, and drink their tea.
We look at them just as the winter night
With its vast empty spaces bends to see
Our isolated little world of light,

Covered with snow, and snow in clouds above it,
And drifts and swirls too deep to understand.
Still, I must try to think a little of it,
With so much winter in my head and hand.

Frozen Drought

Surprising sunshine has ruled more than a hundred days
of this bare winter. Snow has forgotten itself.
The ground lies hard as stone and flat with dust
as though the surface were peeling in the wind
and blowing off to hell or to dust-heaven.
Neighbors and newspapers speak of the oddity,
snowless New England! Week after week blows by
and the ground grows dryer and the teeth grit.
The nose seals up against an invasion
of drought in Eastern air that never tasted
the brown dark of the dust over bleeding Kansas.

Begging for Change in Winter

This season always makes me think of peace,
Or dream of it at least, as I ignore
The signs of its receding from the world:
The headlines' promise of another war,

Or dream of it at least, as I ignore
An unkempt man who begs for change, who keeps
The headlines' promise of another war.
The rich against the poor, it's me against

This unkempt man who begs for change, who keeps
Reminding me of my humanity.
The rich against the poor; it's me against
The forces of injustice, all alone

Reminding me of my humanity,
My coffee burns my tongue. It hurts to drink
The forces of injustice. All alone
In bed last night, I dreamed this happy dream:

My coffee burns my tongue, it hurts to drink
Because I'm nearly dead from thirst and then
In bed—O last of nights!—I dreamed. This dream
Was like my dream of peace, except peace wins

Because there's no one dead from thirst. And then
The world was pure again, receiving gifts
And giving them. I toss the man my change.
This season always makes me question peace.

Foxes in Winter

Every night in the moonlight the foxes come down the hill
to gnaw on the bones of birds. I never said
nature wasn't cruel. Once, in a city as hot as these woods
are cold, I met a boy with a broken face. To stay
alive, he was a beggar. Also, in the night, a thief.
And there are birds in his country that look like rainbows—
if he could have caught them, he would have
torn off their feathers and put their bodies into
his own. The foxes are hungry, who could blame them
for what they do? I never said
we weren't sunk in glittering nature, until we are able
to become something else. As for the boy, it's simple.
He had nothing, not even a bird. All night the pines
are so cold their branches crack. All night the snow falls
softly down. Then it shines like a field
of white flowers. Then it tightens.

Wintering

This is the easy time, there is nothing doing.
I have whirled the midwife's extractor,
I have my honey,
Six jars of it,
Six cat's eyes in the wine cellar,

Wintering in a dark without window
At the heart of the house
Next to the last tenant's rancid jam
And the bottles of empty glitters—
Sir So-and-so's gin.

This is the room I have never been in.
This is the room I could never breathe in.
The black bunched in there like a bat,
No light
But the torch and its faint

Chinese yellow on appalling objects—
Black asininity. Decay.
Possession.
It is they who own me.
Neither cruel nor indifferent,

Only ignorant.
This is the time of hanging on for the bees—the bees
So slow I hardly know them,
Filing like soldiers
To the syrup tin

To make up for the honey I've taken.
Tate and Lyle keeps them going,
The refined snow.
It is Tate and Lyle they live on, instead of flowers.
They take it. The cold sets in.

Now they ball in a mass,
Black
Mind against all that white.
The smile of the snow is white.
It spreads itself out, a mile-long body of Meissen,

Into which, on warm days,
They can only carry their dead.
The bees are all women,
Maids and the long royal lady.
They have got rid of the men,

The blunt, clumsy stumblers, the boors.
Winter is for women—
The woman, still at her knitting,
At the cradle of Spanish walnut,
Her body a bulb in the cold and too dumb to think.

Will the hive survive, will the gladiolas
Succeed in banking their fires
To enter another year?
What will they taste of, the Christmas roses?
The bees are flying. They taste the spring.

ROBERT PACK

Her Black Hair

blows within his dream as lifting snow,
within the snow's descent, begins again.
Upon his window-ledge, he sees two crows.
Laughing asleep, he starts to touch her when
snow swirls the pillow where she lies.
He strains to stroke and wake her with his eyes.

Thrashed snowlight fills their mirror and explodes;
his outstretched body tumbles toward the sun,
traversed by silent, slowly flapping crows.
He strains from sleep to call her once again,
but sees her start. She knows he cannot stop.
The mirror meets them rising as they drop.

Two crows perch on a rigid hemlock limb,
wind glistening their wings as their bills meet.
He dreams he touches her, she touches him;
he hears her in the laughter of his sleep.
The window in the mirror starts to flow
and lifts their rising with the lift of snow.

And now his laughter startles her awake,
and hemlock branches now begin to rise.
Behind the windy mirror two crows break
into the light exploding from his eyes.
Awake to his own starting, she is there—
sun on her arms. He touches her black hair.

Good Hours

I had for my winter evening walk—
No one at all with whom to talk,
But I had the cottages in a row
Up to their shining eyes in snow.

And I thought I had the folk within:
I had the sound of a violin;
I had a glimpse through curtain laces
Of youthful forms and youthful faces.

I had such company outward bound.
I went till there were no cottages found.
I turned and repented, but coming back
I saw no window but that was black.

Over the snow my creaking feet
Disturbed the slumbering village street
Like profanation, by your leave,
At ten o'clock of a winter eve.

On New Year's Day

Bless this my house under the pitch pines
where the cardinal flashes and the kestrels hover
crying, where I live and work with my lover
Woody and my cats, where the birds gather
in winter to be fed and the squirrel dines
from the squirrel-proof feeder. Keep our water
bubbling up clear. Protect us from the fire's
long teeth and the lashing of the hurricanes
and the government. Please, no foreign wars.
Keep this house from termites and the bane
of quarreling past what can be sweetly healed.
Keep our cats from hunters and savage dogs.
Watch with care over Woody splitting logs
and mostly keep us from our sharpening fear
as we skate over the ice of the new year.

from "Snow-Bound"

The sun that brief December day
Rose cheerless over hills of gray,
And, darkly circled, gave at noon
A sadder light than waning moon.
Slow tracing down the thickening sky
Its mute and ominous prophecy,
A portent seeming less than threat,
It sank from sight before it set.
A chill no coat, however stout,
Of homespun stuff could quite shut out,
A hard, dull bitterness of cold,
The checked, mid-vein, the circling race
Of life-blood in the sharpened face,
The coming of the snow-storm told.
The wind blew east; we heard the roar
Of Ocean on his wintry shore,
And felt the strong pulse throbbing there
Beat with low rhythm our inland air.

Meanwhile we did our nightly chores,—
Brought in the wood from out of doors,
Littered the stalls, and from the mows
Raked down the herd's-grass for the cows:
Heard the horse whinnying for his corn;
And, sharply clashing horn on horn,
Impatient down the stanchion rows

The cattle shake their walnut bows;
While, peering from his early perch
Upon the scaffold's pole of birch,
The cock his crested helmet bent
And down his querulous challenge sent.

Unwarmed by any sunset light
The gray day darkened into night,
A night made hoary with the swarm
And whirl-dance of the blinding storm,
As zigzag, wavering to and fro,
Crossed and recrossed the winged snow:
And ere the early bedtime came
The white drift piled the window-frame,
And through the glass the clothes-line posts
Looked in like tall and sheeted ghosts.

So all night long the storm roared on:
The morning broke without a sun;
In tiny spherule traced with lines
Of Nature's geometric signs,
In starry flake, and pellicle,
All day the hoary meteor fell;
And, when the second morning shone,
We looked upon a world unknown,
On nothing we could call our own.
Around the glistening wonder bent
The blue walls of the firmament,
No cloud above, no earth below,—
A universe of sky and snow!

From a Notebook

The whiteness near and far.
The cold, the hush . . .
A first word stops
The blizzard, steps
Out into fresh
Candor. You ask no more.

Each never taken stride
Leads onward, though
In circles ever
Smaller, smaller.
The vertigo
Upholds you. And now to glide

Across the frozen pond,
Steelshod, to chase
Its dreamless oval
With loop and spiral
Until (your face
Downshining, lidded, drained

Of any need to know
What hid, what called,
Wisdom or error,

Beneath that mirror)
The page you scrawled
Turns. A new day. Fresh snow.

Notes on a Blizzard

Snow makes Monday as white
at supper as breakfast was.
All day I watch for our wild
turkeys, the ones you've tamed
with horse corn, but only the old
one comes, toeing out on his henna feet.
Small-headed, pot-bellied, he stands
too tall—I need to think this—
to tempt a raccoon. Tonight, not
turning once, I sleep in your empty space
as simply as a child in a child's cot.

Tuesday, the sky still spits
its fancywork. Wherever
the chickadees swim to is secret.
The house breathes, you occur to me as
that cough in the chimney, that phlegm-fall
while the wood fire steams, hard put
to keep itself from going out.

Wednesday, the phone's dead.
The dog coils his clay tail across
his eyes and runs, closing in
on a rabbit. Late afternoon,
in a lull, I go out on snowshoes

to look the woods over.
Above the brook a deer
is tearing bark from a birch tree,
as hungry as that, tearing
it off in strips the way
you might string celery.

Thursday, the wind turns. We're down
to snow squalls now. Last night you walked
barefoot into my dream. The mice
wrangling on all sides
raised thunder in my head,
nothing but lathe and plaster
between them and the weather.

It's Friday. The phone works.
You're driving north. Your voice
is faint, as if borne across
clothesline and tin cans from the treehouse.
The turkeys show up again
flopping under the kitchen window
like novice swimmers daring the deep end.
Low on corn, I offer jelly beans.
The sun somes out eventually,
a bedded woman, one
surprised eye open.

Snow-Flakes

Out of the bosom of the Air,
    Out of the cloud-folds of her garments shaken,
Over the woodlands brown and bare,
    Over the harvest-fields forsaken,
        Silent, and soft, and slow
        Descends the snow.

Even as our cloudy fancies take
    Suddenly shape in some divine expression,
Even as the troubled heart doth make
    In the white countenance confession,
        The troubled sky reveals
        The grief it feels.

This is the poem of the air,
    Slowly in silent syllables recorded;
This is the secret of despair,
    Long in its cloudy bosom hoarded,
        Now whispered and revealed
        To wood and field.

EMILY DICKINSON

Snow flakes

Snow flakes.
I counted till they danced so
Their slippers leaped the town,
And then I took a pencil
To note the rebels down.
And then they grew so jolly
I did resign the prig,
And ten of my once stately toes
Are marshalled for a jig!

Walking Alone in Late Winter

How long the winter has lasted—like a Mahler
symphony, or an hour in the dentist's chair.
In the fields the grasses are matted
and gray, making me think of June, when hay
and vetch burgeon in the heat, and warm rain
swells the globed buds of the peony.

Ice on the pond breaks into huge planes. One
sticks like a barge gone away at the neck
of the bridge. . . . The reeds
and shrubby brush along the shore
gleam with ice that shatters when breeze
moves them. From beyond the bog
the sound of water rushing over trees
felled by the zealous beavers,
who bring them crashing down. . . . Sometimes
it seems they do it just for fun.

Those days of anger and remorse
come back to me; you fidgeting with your ring,
sliding it off, then jabbing it on again.

The wind is keen coming over the ice;
it carries the sound of breaking glass.
And the sun, bright but not warm,
has gone behind the hill. Chill, or the fear
of chill, sends me hurrying home.

The Snow

Snow is in the oak.
Behind the thick, whitening
air which the wind drives,
the weight of the sun
presses the snow
on the pane of my window.

I remember snows and walking
through their first fall in cities,
asleep or drunk
with the slow, desperate falling.
The snow blurs in my eyes,
with other snows.

Snow is what must
come down, even if it struggles
to stay in the air with the strength
of the wind. Like an old man,
whatever I touch I turn
to the story of death.

Snow is what fills
the oak, and what covers
the grass and the bare garden.
Snow is what reverses

sidewalk, house and lawn
into the substance of whiteness.

So the watcher sleeps himself
back to the baby's eyes.
The tree, the breast, and the floor
are limbs of him, and from
his eyes he extends a skin
which grows over the world.

The baby is what must
have fallen, like snow. He resisted,
the way the old man
struggles inside the airy tent
to keep on breathing.
Birth is the fear of death

and the source of an old hope.
Snow is what melts. I distrust
the cycles of water.
The sun has withdrawn itself
and the snow keeps falling,
and something will always be falling.

Snow, snow

Like the sun on February ice dazzling;
like the sun licking the snow back
roughly so objects begin to poke through,
logs and steps, withered clumps of herb;
like the torch of the male cardinal
borne across the clearing from pine
to pine and then lighting among the bird
seed and bread scattered; like the sharp
shinned hawk gliding over the rabbit
colored marsh grass, exulting
in talon-hooked cries to his larger mate;
like the little pale green seedlings sticking
up their fragile heavy heads on white stalks
into the wide yellow lap of the pregnant sun;
like the sky of stained glass the eye seeks
for respite from the glitter that makes the lips
part; similar to all of these pleasures
of the failing winter and the as yet unbroken
blue egg of spring is our joy as we twist
and twine about each other in the bed
facing the window where the sun plays
the tabla of the thin cold air
and the snow sings soprano
and the emerging earth drones bass.

The Wood-Pile

Out walking in the frozen swamp one gray day,
I paused and said, 'I will turn back from here.
No, I will go on farther—and we shall see.'
The hard snow held me, save where now and then
One foot went through. The view was all in lines
Straight up and down of tall slim trees
Too much alike to mark or name a place by
So as to say for certain I was here
Or somewhere else: I was just far from home.
A small bird flew before me. He was careful
To put a tree between us when he lighted,
And say no word to tell me who he was
Who was so foolish as to think what *he* thought.
He thought that I was after him for a feather—
The white one in his tail; like one who takes
Everything said as personal to himself.
One flight out sideways would have undeceived him.
And then there was a pile of wood for which
I forgot him and let his little fear
Carry him off the way I might have gone,
Without so much as wishing him good-night.
He went behind it to make his last stand.
It was a cord of maple, cut and split
And piled—and measured, four by four by eight.
And not another like it could I see.

No runner tracks in this year's snow looped near it.
And it was older sure than this year's cutting,
Or even last year's or the year's before.
The wood was gray and the bark warping off it
And the pile somewhat sunken. Clematis
Had wound strings round and round it like a bundle.
What held it though on one side was a tree
Still growing, and on one a stake and prop,
These latter about to fall. I thought that only
Someone who lived in turning to fresh tasks
Could so forget his handiwork on which
He spent himself, the labor of his ax,
And leave it there far from a useful fireplace
To warm the frozen swamp as best it could
With the slow smokeless burning of decay.

Crows

It is January, and there are the crows
like black flowers on the snow.
While I watch they rise and float toward the frozen pond,
    they have seen
some streak of death on the dark ice.
They gather around it and consume everything, the strings
and the red music of that nameless body. Then they shout,
one hungry, blunt voice echoing another.
It begins to rain.
Later, it becomes February,
and even later, spring
returns, a chorus of thousands.
They bow, and begin their important music.
I recognize the oriole.
I recognize the thrush, and the mockingbird.
I recognize the business of summer, which is to forge ahead,
    delicately.
So I dip my fingers among the green stems, delicately.
I lounge at the edge of the leafing pond, delicately.
I scarcely remember the crust of the snow.
I scarcely remember the icy dawns and the sun like a lamp
    without a fuse.
I don't remember the fury of loneliness.
I never felt the wind's drift.
I never heard of the struggle between anything and nothing.
I never saw the flapping, blood-gulping crows.

The Snow-Storm

Announced by all the trumpets of the sky,
Arrives the snow, and, driving o'er the fields,
Seems nowhere to alight: the whited air
Hides hills and woods, the river, and the heaven,
And veils the farm-house at the garden's end.
The sled and traveller stopped, the courier's feet
Delayed, all friends shut out, the housemates sit
Around the radiant fireplace, enclosed
In a tumultuous privacy of storm.

Come see the north wind's masonry.
Out of an unseen quarry evermore
Furnished with tile, the fierce artificer
Curves his white bastions with projected roof
Round every windward stake, or tree, or door.
Speeding, the myriad-handed, his wild work
So fanciful, so savage, nought cares he
For number or proportion. Mockingly,
On coop or kennel he hangs Parian wreaths;
A swan-like form invests the hidden thorn;
Fills up the farmer's lane from wall to wall,
Maugre the farmer's sighs; and at the gate
A tapering turret overtops the work.
And when his hours are numbered, and the world
Is all his own, retiring, as he were not,

Leaves, when the sun appears, astonished Art
To mimic in slow structures, stone by stone,
Built in an age, the mad wind's night-work,
The frolic architecture of the snow.

ANNE SEXTON

Landscape Winter

Snow, out over the elephant's rump,
my rock outside my word-window,
where it lies in a doze on the front lawn.
Oak leaves, each separate and pink
in the setting sun, as good cows' tongues.
The snow far off on the pine
nesting into the needles
like addicts into their fix.
The mailbox as stiff as a soldier
but wearing a chef's hat.
The ground is full.
It will not eat any more.
Armies of angels have sunk onto it
with their soft parachutes.

And within the house
ashes are being stuffed into my marriage,
fury is lapping the walls,
dishes crack on the shelves,
a strangler needs my throat,
the daughter has ceased to eat anything,
the wife speaks of this
but only the ice cubes listen.

The sweat of fear pumps inside me.
In my sleep I wet the bed,
the marriage bed,
three nights in a row
and soon, soon I'd better run out
while there is time.

Yet, right now,
the outside world seems oblivious
and the snow is happy and all is quiet
as the night waits for its breakfast.

ANNE BRADSTREET

Winter

Cold, moist, young phlegmy Winter now doth lie
In swaddling clouts, like newborn infancy,
Bound up with frosts, and furred with hail and snows,
And like an infant, still it taller grows;
December is my first, and now the sun
To th' Southward tropic, his swift race doth run:
This month he's housed in horned Capricorn,
From thence he 'gins to length the shortned morn,
Through Christendom with great festivity,
Now's held (but guest), for blest Nativity.
Cold frozen January next comes in,
Chilling the blood and shrinking up the skin;
In Aquarius now keeps the long wisht sun,
And Northward his unwearied course doth run:
The day much longer then it was before,
The cold not lessened, but augmented more.
Now toes and ears, and fingers often freeze,
And travelers their noses sometimes leese.
Moist snowy February is my last,
I care not how the winter time doth haste.
In Pisces now the golden sun doth shine,
And Northward still approaches to the line,
The rivers 'gin to ope, the snows to melt,
And some warm glances from his face are felt;

Which is increased by the lengthened day,
Until by's heat, he drive all cold away,
And thus the year in circle runneth round:
Where first it did begin, in th' end it's found.

Boleros #36

The poplars have grown their winter cotton,
snow that winds a shaggy warmth around the branches.
At night now, even when the moon has tucked itself
into its patchy quilt,
you can go from this house in the hollow
to the house at the point of the stone wall,
following the trees' light and silence
through fog that inexplicably rises
                                    and suddenly disappears.
White seams in the lapis lazuli skirt of a New
Hampshire night remind us of the first time
we saw the aluminum shimmy of northern lights,
the hants' tree houses,
from which, through the fluttering doors,
we expected to hear an *hechicera* voice
and the *montuno* of a home we had swiftly
                                    abandoned.

There is another voice,
high in the White Mountains,
one we carried in your father's urn
from appleless Jersey and scattered
in the moss shadow of a singular apple tree.
In spring,

it comes in the white-throated sparrow's song,
a melisma of misery tempered by the thrill of survival.

Soon, the mauve summer sky
will strike its evening tympanum,
and move you through the deep waters of wonder
                              into a forgiving sleep.

RICHARD WILBUR

Boy at the Window

Seeing the snowman standing all alone
In dusk and cold is more than he can bear.
The small boy weeps to hear the wind prepare
A night of gnashings and enormous moan.
His tearful sight can hardly reach to where
The pale-faced figure with bitumen eyes
Returns him such a god-forsaken stare
As outcast Adam gave to Paradise.

The man of snow is, nonetheless, content,
Having no wish to go inside and die.
Still, he is moved to see the youngster cry.
Though frozen water is his element,
He melts enough to drop from one soft eye
A trickle of the purest rain, a tear
For the child at the bright pane surrounded by
Such warmth, such light, such love, and so much fear.

". . . and they that know the winters of that country know them to be sharp and violent, and subject to cruel and fierce storms," wrote William Bradford of the new land a leaky *Mayflower* had brought him to in 1620. The Puritan poet **Anne Bradstreet** (c. 1612–1672) was also painfully familiar with New England winter, that long season she closely identifies with illness, adversity, separation, and mortality. Born in Northampton, England, she married the Cambridge graduate Simon Bradstreet when she was fourteen and he twenty-five. Two years later in 1630, she accompanied him to Massachusetts, where they eventually settled in North Andover. The busy mother of eight would become the first New England colonist to publish a volume of poetry when *The Tenth Muse Lately Sprung Up in America* appeared in England in 1650.

Born in Dover, New Jersey, in 1964, **Rafael Campo** is the author of *Landscape with Human Figure* (2002); *Diva* (1999), a finalist for the National Book Critics Circle Award; *What the Body Told* (1996), winner of a Lambda Literary Award; and *The Other Man Was Me: A Voyage to the New World* (1994), winner of the National Poetry Series 1993 Open Competition. He also received a Lambda Literary Award for Memoir for an essay collection, *The Poetry of Healing* (1996). Other awards include the National Hispanic Academy of Arts and Sciences Annual Achievement Award, and fellowships from the Guggenheim Foundation and the Echoing Green Foundation. He is a practicing physician at Harvard Medical School and the Beth Israel Deaconess Medical Center in Boston.

Peter Davison was born in New York City in 1928. After receiving his education at Harvard and Cambridge University, Davison took a series of editorial positions at Harcourt, Brace, Harvard University Press, and then the Atlantic Monthly Press, where he served for nearly thirty years, becoming editor-in-chief and director. He has been associated with *The Atlantic Monthly* for over fifty years. In 1964 his first book, *The Breaking of the Day,* was selected for the Yale Series of Younger Poets; other collections include: *Dark Houses* (1971), *A Voice in the Mountain* (1977), and most recently, *Breathing Room* (2000). An autobiography, *Half Remembered: A Personal History,* was published in 1973. "Frozen Drought" is part of a series of poems called "Wordless Winter" that appears in *Barn Fever and Other Poems* (1981).

Emily Dickinson (1830–1886) spent practically her entire life as a recluse in her parents' home in Amherst, Massachusetts, where her father served as treasurer of Amherst College. Although she wrote nearly two thousand poems, only a few were published in her lifetime. The first complete and textually authentic collection of her poetry did not appear until 1955, a publishing event that surely qualifies her as one of America's leading "modern" poets. Through uncanny paths of perception and with remarkable compression, her poems, like momentary flashes of insight, take us to the edges of human thought. Yet, as enigmatic as these mental journeys may seem, they are firmly rooted in a particular place: "I see—New Englandly—," she once rhymed.

America's greatest essayist and one of its most influential thinkers, **Ralph Waldo Emerson** (1803–1882) eventually persuaded himself that prose—not poetry—was his literary gift. Some of Emerson's finest poems, including "The Snow-Storm," were first written out as prose and later tweaked into verse. Though today his poetry is cited far less frequently than the essays, it has nonetheless attracted many ardent admirers ever since his first volume, *Poems,* appeared in 1847. Robert Frost carried a first edition around with him and knew the poems intimately, considering one of them ("Uriel") "the best Western poem yet." Born in Boston, Emerson moved into the family home in Concord, Massachusetts, in 1834 and would reside there for the remainder of his life. He wrote "The Snow-Storm" shortly after his move to Concord.

So associated is he with the New England landscape (and his name with its weather) that few people realize that **Robert Frost** (1874–1963) was actually born in San Francisco. He didn't move east until he was eleven, when his father's death left the family penniless. Snowy winter evenings figure prominently throughout Frost's poetry and such isolated moments seem to be one of his chief sources of inspiration. To call special attention to it, he deliberately set "Good Hours" in italics and put it at the end of his second volume of poetry, *North of Boston* (1916). Though little known, "Good Hours" prefigures such later snow poems as "Stopping by Woods on a Snowy Evening," which was purposely not selected for this collection, since most readers apparently know it by heart.

Angelina Weld Grimké (1880–1958) is best known as the author of *Rachel* (1916), one of the first successful African American plays with an all-black cast. The daughter of a Harvard-educated African American lawyer and a prominent white Boston woman, Grimké was permanently abandoned by her mother, who could not withstand the social pressure of her interracial marriage, and raised solely by her father, who provided her with a solid private school education. Though she published poetry in some of the leading periodicals and anthologies connected with the Harlem Renaissance, her work remained uncollected until Carolivia Herron edited the *Selected Works of Angelina Weld Grimké* in 1991.

One of the nation's most versatile literary figures, **Donald Hall** was born in New Haven, Connecticut, in 1928, and is the author of numerous books of poetry, fiction, essays, memoir, and criticism, as well as the editor of many influential textbooks and anthologies. After graduation from Harvard in 1951, Hall received a B. Litt. from Oxford in 1953, the same year he became poetry editor of the newly founded *Paris Review*. His first collection, *Exiles and Marriages,* appeared in 1955. Hall left the University of Michigan, where he was an English professor, and moved to a family farm in New Hampshire after his marriage to Jane Kenyon (see below) in 1972. *Without: Poems* (1998) commemorates her death from leukemia in 1995. Other recent poetry collections include: *The Painted Bed* (2002); *Old and New Poems* (1990); *The One Day* (1988), which won the National Book Critics Circle Award; and *The Happy Man* (1986), which won the Lenore Marshall Poetry Prize. His highly popular children's book *Ox-Cart Man* (1979) won the Caldecott Medal. The recipient of two Guggenheim fellowships and the Poetry Society of America's Robert Frost Silver medal, Hall lives in Danbury, New Hampshire.

Born in 1947 in Ann Arbor, Michigan, **Jane Kenyon** graduated in 1970 from the University of Michigan, where she received an M.A. in 1972, the same year she married the poet Donald Hall, whom she had met as a student. They moved to Eagle Pond Farm in New Hampshire. Kenyon is the author of several volumes of poetry: *Constance* (1993), *Let Evening Come* (1990), *The Boat of Quiet Hours* (1986), and *From Room to Room* (1978). Her translation, *Twenty Poems of Anna Akhmatova,* was published in 1985. She was New Hampshire's poet laureate when she died of leukemia in 1995. *Otherwise: New and Selected Poems* appeared in 1996.

A longtime New Hampshire resident, where she raises horses and vegetables, **Maxine Kumin** was born in Philadelphia in 1925 and educated at Radcliffe College. Her books of poetry include: *Connecting the Dots* (1996); *Looking for Luck* (1992); *Nurture* (1989); *The Long Approach* (1986); *Our Ground Time Here Will Be Brief* (1982); *House, Bridge, Fountain, Gate* (1975); and the Pulitzer Prize–winning *Up Country: Poems of New England* (1972). Besides novels, short stories, and several essay collections, she has also written many books for children. A Poet Laureate of New Hampshire, she has received an American Academy of Arts and Letters Award, a National Endowment for the Arts grant, and fellowships from The Academy of American Poets and the National Council on the Arts. Her memoir *Inside the Halo and Beyond: The Anatomy of a Recovery* was published in 2000. "Notes on a Blizzard" is from *The Retrieval Season* (1978).

In mid-nineteenth-century America there was no poet more popular or more respected than **Henry Wadsworth Longfellow** (1807–1882), whose first volume of poetry, *Voices of the Night* (1837), achieved best-seller status before such lists existed. His poems were so well known to the public that parodies often supplied amusing advertising copy. Born in Portland, Maine, Longfellow studied modern languages at Bowdoin College (Nathaniel Hawthorne was a classmate) and continued in that field at Harvard, where in 1836 he became a professor, though his astonishing literary success enabled him to resign his position in 1854. Longfellow acquired a formidable reputation in England and remains the only non-British literary figure to be honored in Poet's Corner, Westminster Abbey.

A relative of James Russell Lowell, **Amy Lowell** (1874–1925) was born in Brookline, Massachusetts, the sister of Abbott Lawrence Lowell, who would serve as Harvard University's president for nearly twenty-five years. Influenced by the Imagist movement, she began publishing experimental and highly visual poems beginning with *Sword Blades and Poppy Seed* (1914). She became a leading and controversial advocate of the "New Poetry," which she helped promote through criticism, theatrical lecture tours, and collections. Her spirited but disorganized biographical study of John Keats appeared just before her untimely death. Though she received a posthumous Pulitzer Prize for her last volume of poetry, she remains a neglected literary figure, despite the recent attention given to her work by feminist critics as well as scholars of gay and lesbian studies.

One of the leading members of the Boston "Brahmin caste," **James Russell Lowell** (1819–1891) was born into a distinguished Cambridge family. After making a name for himself as an undergraduate poet at Harvard, Lowell took a law degree, but his career quickly veered off toward literature after the success of his first book of poetry in 1841. A prolific and versatile writer, Lowell is best known today for two long satirical poems, both published in 1848: *The Bigelow Papers* and *A Fable for Critics*. During this period, Lowell's life was devastated by the loss of his wife, his mother, and three of his children, one of which is the subject of "The First Snow-Fall." Of this touching poem, Lowell wrote to his editor: "May you never have the key which shall unlock the whole meaning of the poem to you."

Born in New York City, **James Merrill** (1926–1995) was the son of the founder of the Merrill Lynch investment firm. Merrill, who had been composing poems while a teenager at the Lawrenceville School, continued his interests at Amherst, and a few years after graduation received the Yale Younger Poets award from W. H. Auden for *First Poems* (1951). Although he traveled widely and owned places in Athens and Key West, Merrill in the mid-fifties settled in Stonington, Connecticut, with his companion, and lived there his entire life. Merrill's poetry has won many awards, including a National Book Award for *Nights and Days* (1966), the Bollingen Award for *Braving the Elements* (1972), a Pulitzer Prize for *Divine Comedies* (1976), and the National Book Critics Circle Award for *The Changing Light at Sandover* (1982). "From a Notebook" is from *Water Street* (1962), a volume that reflects his move to the house located on that street in Stonington.

Mary Oliver was born in 1935 in Maple Heights, Ohio. Her many books include *Winter Hours: Prose, Prose Poems, and Poems* (1999); *West Wind* (1997); *White Pine* (1994); *New and Selected Poems* (1992), winner of the National Book award; *House of Light* (1990), winner of the Christopher Award and the L. L. Winship/PEN New England Award; and *American Primitive* (1983), which won the Pulitzer Prize. She has also written *Rules for the Dance: A Handbook for Writing and Reading Metrical Verse* (1998); *Blue Pastures* (1995); and *A Poetry Handbook* (1994). She has received an American Academy of Arts and Letters Award, a Lannan Literary Award, and fellowships from the Guggenheim Foundation and the National Endowment for the Arts. She holds the Catharine Osgood Foster Chair for Distinguished Teaching at Bennington College.

The author of numerous books of poetry, **Robert Pack** was born in New York City in 1929. His most recent volumes include: *Rounding It Out* (1999), *Minding the Sun* (1996), and *Fathering the Map* (1993). His first collection, *The Irony of Joy*, appeared in 1955 and two years later he edited with Donald Hall (see above) the enormously influential anthology *The New Poets of England and America*. In 1980 he published one of his most highly acclaimed volumes, *Waking to My Name: New and Selected Poems*. Pack has taught at Middlebury College for many years and has been director of the Bread Loaf Writers' Conference. His reviews and essays have appeared nationwide, and his study of Wallace Stevens (1958) stands as one of the earliest critical books on that poet. In 1994, Pack received the Dartmouth College medal for accomplishment and leadership. "Her Black Hair" is from *Nothing but Light* (1972).

Marge Piercy was born in Detroit, Michigan, in 1936. After graduating from the University of Michigan, she earned a master's degree from Northwestern University. Her many books of poetry include *The Art of Blessing the Day: Poems with a Jewish Theme* (1999), *Early Grrrl: The Early Poems of Marge Piercy* (1999), *What Are Big Girls Made Of?* (1997), *Mars and Her Children* (1992), *Available Light* (1988), *Circles on the Water: Selected Poems of Marge Piercy* (1982), and *The Moon Is Always Female* (1980). She has written fifteen novels, most recently *Three Women* (1999), *City of Darkness, City of Light* (1996), *The Longings of Women* (1994), and *He, She and It* (1991). In 1998, she coauthored a novel, *Storm Tide,* with her husband, Ira Wood. She lives in Wellfleet, Massachusetts.

Sylvia Plath (1932–1963) was born in Boston and, despite suicidal bouts of depression, performed outstandingly at Smith College, where she graduated not only with highest honors but also with a portfolio of impressive literary prizes and publications. While on a Fulbright to Cambridge she secretly married the poet Ted Hughes in 1956. They had two children, but after discovering his infidelity, she separated and in December 1962 moved with the children into a London flat, where, depressed beyond psychiatric help, she took her life a few months later. Nearly all her major work was published posthumously, including her finest volume, *Ariel* (1965), which features the intense poetry she wrote in the desolate months before her death. "Wintering" appears there among a series of poems that derive their furious imagery from childhood memories of her father, a Boston University zoology professor who studied bees.

Born in 1953 in Tacoma, Washington, **Gjertrud Schnackenberg** is a graduate of Mount Holyoke College and the author of several award-winning volumes of poetry, including *Portraits and Elegies* (1982), *The Lamplit Answer* (1985), *A Gilded Lapse of Time* (1992), and *The Throne of Labdacus* (2000). Her first three books were collected in *Supernatural Love: Poems, 1978–1992.* She has been awarded fellowships from the Guggenheim Foundation, the National Endowment for the Arts, the Bunting Institute at Radcliffe College, and the Ingram Merrill Foundation, and has received the Rome Prize in Literature and an Award in Literature from the American Academy of Arts and Letters. "The Paperweight" is part of a sequence of poems, "19 Hadley Street," that forms a major part of *Portraits and Elegies.*

Anne Sexton (1928–1974) was born in Newton, Massachusetts, and spent her entire life in the Boston vicinity. As a young woman she briefly modeled and—not possessing a college degree—studied poetry in adult education workshops, where she met Maxine Kumin (see above), who would be a lifelong friend. Married at the age of twenty, she went through years of therapy with occasional institutionalization after several devastating mental breakdowns in the mid-fifties, stark experiences that form the core of her first award-winning volume of poetry, *To Bedlam and Part Way Back* (1960). Her stability worsened after her divorce in 1973 and not long afterward she committed suicide. "Winter Landscape" grows out of those last days and forms a section of the posthumously published *45 Mercy Street* (1976) called "The Divorce Papers."

Born in 1938, **Charles Simic** came to the United States with his family from Belgrade, Yugoslavia, in 1949, having witnessed as a child the turmoil of World War Two, an indelible experience that continues to shape his poetry and prose. After serving in the Army (1961-63), Simic graduated from New York University and published his first volume of poetry, *What the Grass Says*, in 1967. Other titles include: *Dismantling the Silence* (1971), *Return to a Place Lit by a Glass of Milk* (1974), *Charon's Cosmology* (1977), *Classic Ballroom Dances* (1980), *Unending Blues* (1986), *Selected Poems* (1985), and *A Wedding in Hell* (1994). The recipient of a Mac-Arthur Fellowship along with many other awards, Simic won a Pulitzer Prize in 1990 for a collection of prose poems, *The World Doesn't End*. Simic lives in New Hampshire.

Though he wrote many winter poems, **Wallace Stevens** (1879–1955) created his most haunting with "The Snow Man," which inspired both the title and theme of this collection—and which appropriately opens it. Born in Reading, Pennsylvania, Stevens attended Harvard and, after completing his law degree in New York, began a successful career as an insurance executive in Hartford, Connecticut, where he lived from 1916 until his death. One of his earliest published poems, "The Snow Man" was written around the time of his move to Connecticut and was included in his first book, *Harmonium* (1923), which remains one of the most impressive first volumes of poetry in American literary history.

Rosanna Warren was born in Fairfield, Connecticut, in 1953. Her volumes of poetry include *Stained Glass* (1993), *Each Leaf Shines Separate* (1984), and *Snow Day* (1981). Her translation (with Stephen Scully) of Euripides's *Suppliant Women* appeared in 1995. The recipient of many awards, including the Ingram Merrill Foundation Award, a Lila Wallace–Reader's Digest

Award, and fellowships from the Guggenheim Foundation and the American Council of Learned Societies, she is currently Emma MacLachlan Metcalf Professor of the Humanities at Boston University.

For several generations, **John Greenleaf Whittier** (1807–1892) was considered the premier poet of rural New England, and his idyllic "Snow-Bound," completed soon after the Civil War in 1865, remained a classroom classic well into the 1950s, its melodious opening lines assigned year after year for memorization and recitation. Born into a poor Quaker family near Haverhill, Massachusetts, Whittier devoted his poetic talents for several decades to the abolitionist movement, a cause he held dearly. Only after Emancipation did he feel comfortable turning to more literary themes and purposes. At the time of his death, he was revered as one of America's preeminent authors. "Snow-Bound," which begins with an epigraph from Emerson's "The Snow-Storm," is 759 lines long; only the opening is reprinted here.

Verbally polished until they shine, **Richard Wilbur**'s poems have served as models of the poet's craft ever since *The Beautiful Changes and Other Poems* appeared in 1947. One would be hard-pressed to find a reputable textbook on the art of poetry that did not include a few examples of Wilbur's disciplined and exemplary work. Born in New York City in 1921, Wilbur was educated at Amherst College (where he studied with Robert Frost) and Harvard University. America's Poet Laureate in 1987, Wilbur won the Pulitzer Prize in 1989 for his *New and Collected Poems*. He has taught for many years at Wesleyan University and is also well known for his highly acclaimed translations of Molière.

Jay Wright was born in Albuquerque, New Mexico, in 1935. He is the author of numerous volumes of poetry, including *Transfigurations: Collected Poems* (2000), *Boleros* (1991), *Selected Poems of Jay Wright* (1987), *Explications/Interpretations* (1984), *Elaine's Book* (1986), *The Double Invention of Komo* (1980), *Dimensions of History* (1976), *Soothsayers and Omens* (1976), and *The Homecoming Singer* (1971). He has received an American Academy and Institute of Arts and Letters Literary Award, a Guggenheim Fellowship, a MacArthur Fellowship, an Ingram Merrill Foundation Award, a National Endowment for the Arts grant, a Rockefeller Brothers Theological Fellowship, and the Oscar Williams and Gene Derwood Award. Named a Fellow of the Academy of American Poets in 1995, Wright lives in Bradford, Vermont.

CREDITS

Rafael Campo:
From *Diva* by Rafael Campo. Copyright © 1999 by Rafael Campo.
Reprinted by permission of Duke University Press.

Peter Davison:
From *Barn Fever and Other Poems* by Peter Davison.
Copyright © 1981 by Peter Davison. Reprinted by permission of the author.

Emily Dickinson:
Reprinted by permission of the publishers and the Trustees of Amherst College from *The Poems of Emily Dickinson,* Thomas H. Johnson, ed., Cambridge, Mass.: The Belknap Press of Harvard University Press, Copyright © 1951, 1955, 1979 by the President and Fellows of Harvard College.

Donald Hall:
"The Snow" from *Old and New Poems* by Donald Hall. Copyright © 1990 by Donald Hall. Reprinted by permission of Houghton Mifflin Company. All rights reserved.

Jane Kenyon:
"Walking Alone in Late Winter" copyright © 1996 by the Estate of Jane Kenyon. Reprinted from *Otherwise: New and Selected Poems* with the permission of Graywolf Press, Saint Paul, Minnesota.

Maxine Kumin:
"Notes on a Blizzard" copyright © 1993 by Maxine Kumin.
Reprinted by permission of the author.

James Merrill:
From *Collected Poems* by James Merrill, J. D. McClatchy and Stephen Yenser, editors, copyright © 2001 by the Literary Estate of James Merrill at Washington University. Used by permission of Alfred A. Knopf, a division of Random House, Inc.

Robert Pack:
From *Waking to My Name,* p. 127. © 1980.
Reprinted by permission of the Johns Hopkins University Press.

Marge Piercy:
From *Stone, Paper, Knife* by Marge Piercy, copyright © 1983 by Marge Piercy. Used by permission of Alfred A. Knopf, a division of Random House, Inc.

Sylvia Plath:
All lines from "Wintering" from *Ariel* by Sylvia Plath. Copyright © 1963 by Ted Hughes. Reprinted by permission of HarperCollins Publishers, Inc.